HURRICANE KATRINA
SURVIVAL STORIES

BY JEANNE MARIE FORD

The Child's World®
childsworld.com

Published by The Child's World®
1980 Lookout Drive • Mankato, MN 56003-1705
800-599-READ • www.childsworld.com

Acknowledgments
The Child's World®: Mary Berendes, Publishing Director
Red Line Editorial: Design, editorial direction, and production
Photographs ©: David J. Phillip/AP Images, cover, 1, 28; Jeff Schmaltz/MODIS
Rapid Response Team/NASA/GSFC, 6; Cheryl Gerber/AP Images, 8; LM Otero/AP
Images, 10; Petty Officer 1st Class Mariana O'leary/U.S. Coast Guard, 12; Phil Coale/
AP Images, 14; Dimitrios Kambouris/WireImage for Conde Nast Publications/FPC
Magazines/Getty Images, 16; Public Domain, 17; John Bazemore/AP Images, 18; Eric
Gay/AP Images, 20; NOAA/The COMET Program, 21; Dave Martin/AP Images, 23, 24;
Francisco Bustos/Newscom, 26; NOAA, 27

ISBN 9781634074216

LCCN 2015946310

Printed in the United States of America
Mankato, MN
December, 2015
PA02288

ABOUT THE AUTHOR

Jeanne Marie Ford is an Emmy-winning TV scriptwriter and holds a master
of fine arts in writing for children from the Vermont College of Fine Arts. She
has written five children's books and numerous articles. A college English
instructor, she lives in Maryland with her husband and two children.

TABLE OF
CONTENTS

DISASTER STRIKES

On August 23, 2005, the sun was shining in New Orleans, Louisiana. Tourists crowded the city as they would on any other day. Hundreds of miles away, in the Gulf of Mexico, a storm had begun to form. But it was too small for anyone to worry about yet.

By August 24, the storm had grown strong enough to be given a name—Katrina. Some areas of Florida got up to 13 inches (33 cm) of rain. Power lines fell and left more than 1 million residents in the dark. Falling trees, high waters, and other dangers caused by the storm killed at least 14 people. Then, the storm passed and went out to sea.

Over the Gulf of Mexico, Katrina got stronger. On Sunday, August 28, Mayor Ray Nagin ordered a **mandatory** evacuation of New Orleans. But the roads became jammed with cars. Many residents could not get out. Buses were sent to take those stuck in the city to the Superdome stadium. At least 10,000 people crammed inside as rain began to fall late in the evening on August 28.

Around 6:00 a.m. on August 29, the **eye** of Hurricane Katrina made **landfall** near New Orleans. When it passed, people thought the worst was over. But the **levees** surrounding the city had been badly damaged. Floodwaters began to rise. Sewage filled the streets. There were 100,000 people trapped in the city. Many had no food or water.

On August 31, the floodwaters stopped rising. Finally, the recovery could begin. From the tragedy and loss of Hurricane Katrina also came many stories of courage.

FAST FACTS

Damage
- Estimated $108 billion
- 70 percent of New Orleans's housing was damaged.

Toll
- 1,833 deaths

Aftermath
- New Orleans's population decreased by more than 50 percent in the months following the storm.
- 62 tornadoes formed as a result of the hurricane.

Chapter 1

DETERMINED TO BE A NEW ORLEANS BABY

New Orleans resident Katy Reckdahl was used to reporting the news, not being part of the story. As Hurricane Katrina approached, the journalist was pregnant with her first baby. When she reached into the freezer for a Popsicle on Saturday, August 27, she felt her first labor pain. She knew the baby would be coming soon.

People in New Orleans were used to big storms. The year before, the city had been evacuated for Hurricane Ivan. But Ivan had missed New Orleans.

As Katrina approached, many of Reckdahl's neighbors packed to leave. But her doctor told her to stay put. If Reckdahl got stuck

◀ **As Hurricane Katrina neared the coast, many people in Louisiana evacuated.**

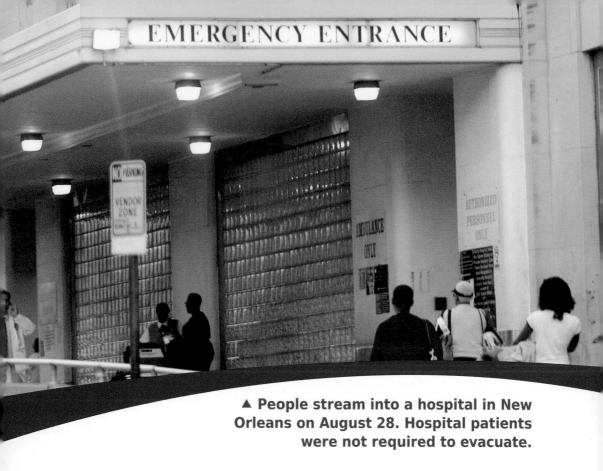

▲ People stream into a hospital in New Orleans on August 28. Hospital patients were not required to evacuate.

in a traffic jam on her way out of the city, her doctor worried she might give birth on the highway.

The baby's father, Merv Campbell, was a professional musician. When he finished his performance that night, he borrowed a car from a friend and drove Reckdahl to the hospital.

Mervin Hector Campbell was born early on August 28. His parents called him Hector. A few hours after Hector was born, Mayor Nagin ordered the whole city to evacuate.

On August 29, Campbell went out to fill up the car's gas tank but could not find a gas station that had any fuel left. Shortly after he returned, the hospital went into a state of lockdown. No one was allowed to leave. Hurricane Katrina hit a little while later. The winds sounded "like a massive freight train," but Reckdahl believed the sturdy hospital was a safe place to be.[1]

When windows began breaking on the upper floors, all the patients' beds were wheeled into the hallways. The power went out, but the **generator** kicked into gear. The storm had passed.

By that night, though, the generator failed. The hospital grew dark, and the temperature rose. Reckdahl struggled to see well enough to change Hector's diaper.

Phones were no longer working, but the hospital had a small radio. The day after the hurricane hit, the new parents heard about flooding in other parts of the city. They realized they might not have an apartment to take their baby home to.

Doctors and nurses volunteered to stay at the hospital. In hospitals throughout the city, very sick patients depended on machines to keep them alive. The machines stopped working when the hospital lost power. Nurses pumped bags to keep air flowing into patients' lungs. With no working elevators, workers carried patients, sometimes down many flights of stairs.

Hospitals were also running out of food. Hector's parents split the small meals that were served. Patients could no longer get the medicine they needed. Floodwater sloshed in the hallways.

▲ Reckdahl and her son celebrate his
first birthday in New Orleans on
August 28, 2006.

On August 31, a doctor told Reckdahl that all the healthy
patients needed to leave right away. "Think of this as a war
situation," he said.[2] But without gas for their vehicle, Reckdahl
and her family could not go anywhere. A nurse finally offered to
drive them to the airport in nearby Baton Rouge. They pushed
their baby in his bassinet out of the hospital. They saw hundreds
of people walking through the flooded streets.

Finally, Reckdahl and her family made it onto a plane bound
for Arizona, where Reckdahl's older sister lived. The pilot made
an announcement that they had a "special passenger" on board:

three-day-old Mervin Hector Campbell. "He was determined to be a New Orleans baby," people told Reckdahl.[3] As soon as they were able, Hector's parents knew they would return to the city to raise their son.

HURRICANE KATRINA TIMELINE

- **August 24: Tropical Storm Katrina develops over the Bahamas.**

- **August 25: Hurricane Katrina moves through southern Florida, knocking out power for more than 1 million residents and killing at least 14 people.**

- **August 28: Katrina grows stronger over the Gulf of Mexico; Mayor Ray Nagin orders an evacuation of New Orleans.**

- **August 29: Katrina makes landfall. The first levee breaks; 20 percent of New Orleans floods.**

- **August 30: Additional levees break; water covers 80 percent of New Orleans. An estimated 100,000 people are still in New Orleans.**

- **August 31: Floodwaters stop rising in New Orleans. Rescue efforts increase.**

Chapter 2

GLAD TO BE THERE TO HELP

As a little girl, Sara Faulkner dreamed of a career where she could help people. She had always been a strong swimmer and thought about joining the navy. Finally, she decided to become one of the first female rescue swimmers in the U.S. Coast Guard. She went through months of long and intense training to achieve her goal.

Faulkner had been in the coast guard for nine years when Hurricane Katrina made landfall. Her unit was waiting in Florida for the storm to pass. Suddenly, they received new orders: "Get airborne immediately. People are dying."[4]

They lifted off and flew into the storm that most people were fleeing from. As the sun came up over Mississippi, Faulkner was shocked by what she saw from the air.

◄ **Faulkner (left) and her crew followed Hurricane Katrina to Mississippi.**

"You could see where winds had ripped the buildings completely apart. You saw buildings pulled out to sea," she said.[5]

Then, over the radio, the rescuers heard one word: "Mayday."

Below was a yacht with three women on it. They had left their flooded house and swam until they found shelter on the abandoned boat.

Faulkner descended from the helicopter in a basket and saw that the oldest woman was going into shock. Faulkner strapped the woman to herself and hoisted her into the helicopter. Faulkner then gave the woman medical treatment on the way to the hospital.

After rescuing another elderly storm victim from a rooftop, Faulkner and her crew refueled. They left Mississippi and headed to Louisiana.

The rescuers scanned the ground below for people who needed help. They saw a balcony with 25 people crowded onto it. As soon as Falkner lowered onto the balcony, a desperate mother reached out and shoved a baby into her arms. Faulkner cradled him carefully as her flight mechanic pulled her back up, spinning and swinging through the air.

The rescuers brought groups of survivors to an evacuation site. When the balcony was clear, they found another group of

◀ **Faulkner performed more than 50 hoists in three days.**

▲ **Faulkner (far right) was named one of *Glamour* magazine's Women of the Year in 2005 for her rescue work during Hurricane Katrina.**

residents on the apartment complex's flooded tennis court. Faulkner and her crew got to work once more.

Faulkner waded into the filthy water and lifted 25 more people, from babies to men much bigger than she was. One man asked if she could take his dog. Faulkner had no way to carry the man's large animal. But she was able to take his small dog and cat.

Faulkner made 52 rescues in three days. For her work, she was recognized as one of *Glamour* magazine's Women of the Year in 2005. "I joined the coast guard to be a rescue swimmer and save lives," Faulkner said. "I was just glad to be there to help in any way I could."[6]

PATH OF DESTRUCTION

Hurricane Katrina began in the Bahamas before sweeping through Florida. As it moved toward the Gulf Coast, it gained speed, reaching wind speeds of more than 170 miles per hour (274 km/h).

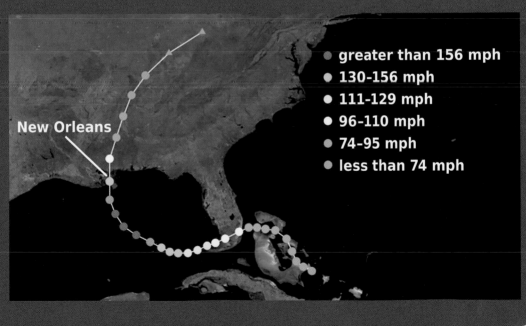

- greater than 156 mph
- 130-156 mph
- 111-129 mph
- 96-110 mph
- 74-95 mph
- less than 74 mph

New Orleans

Chapter 3

THE TREE COPS OF WAVELAND

A scraggly red-tipped bush stands in front of the police department in Waveland, Mississippi. It had been an eyesore for years. The police chief had thought about cutting it down. But he never found the time. His inaction turned out to be a lifesaver.

David and Laura Stepro were married police officers working on the Gulf Coast of Mississippi. As Katrina approached, they decided to stay on the job instead of evacuating.

Laura went to a local store and bought a heavy blue raincoat. The couple dropped off their dog with friends. Then, they both went to their police stations—Laura in Waveland, David in nearby Bay Saint Louis, Mississippi.

In Waveland, police patrolled the streets on Sunday night until the winds grew too strong. Early Monday morning, they went back to the station to wait until the storm passed. The **coastline** was

◀ **High winds ripped through Mississippi on Monday, August 29.**

SPEED LIMIT 35

TO FLORIDA AVE

▲ **Katrina brought extensive flooding throughout the Gulf Coast.**

2 miles (3 km) away. The Waveland police thought they were safe, but they were wrong.

First, the wind rattled the tin station. "We thought the roof might blow off," one officer said.[7] Then, water began to trickle into the back of the building. The officers boarded up the doors. But the **storm surge** kept coming. The water level continued to rise in the station. The chief realized they had to get out. But it was too late. The floodwaters pushed against the front door from the outside. A police car floated against the back door. All 27 people inside the station were trapped.

Buildings around the station were collapsing. Water poured into the building. The soda machine began to float. The officers knew they would die if they stayed where they were. Their only choice was to swim for their lives.

Some of the officers punched a hole through the front door. Water raced in and the officers swam out. They held on to

STORM SURGE

Wind and pressure from a hurricane can make water pile up as it approaches land. This surge of water combines with the height of the normal tide to create a destructively high storm tide.

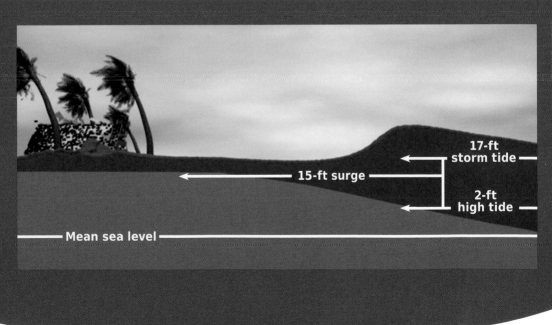

15-ft surge

17-ft storm tide

2-ft high tide

Mean sea level

one another, forming a single file line as they tumbled into the freezing water.

Laura was afraid she would drown as the current started to carry her past the red-tipped bush. Desperate to hang on to something solid, she grabbed it and held tight. She braced both feet against the bush as the water continued to rush by her. Fourteen other officers did the same thing. They clung, they swam, and they waited for help to come.

Meanwhile, the Bay Saint Louis police stayed safe inside their station. All around them, though, businesses were destroyed. The roads in and out of town were completely flooded. The highway bridge collapsed.

As soon as the hurricane's eye passed, David left to find his wife. The water was too deep to drive a car through. Fortunately, he came upon a school bus with the keys still inside. He tried to start it, but its engine sputtered. He tried again. Now, the motor hummed to life. The big bus plowed through the high waters as he drove all the way to Waveland, scanning the side of the road for his wife. Suddenly, he spotted her blue raincoat.

She and the other officers stood on the roadside now. The high waters had passed, but the Waveland officers were drenched and cold. David brought the bus to a halt. He hopped out and ran to Laura. He picked her up and twirled her around.

▲ Flooded roads made it difficult for residents and rescue workers to move around after the storm.

The Stepros lost their home in the storm, but they were grateful to have their lives. Miraculously, all the Waveland police officers survived.

After the storm, the officers gave thanks for that ugly shrub. "I am going to get a sampling from the bush's roots," David said, "and plant one in our new front yard, away from the Gulf of Mexico."[8]

Chapter 4

I SHOULD PLAY
FOR THEM

The Louisiana Superdome was the site of some of the most exciting events in New Orleans history: the Super Bowl, the college basketball championships, many big concerts, and even a visit from the Pope. It was known as a place to go to make special memories.

Samuel Thompson had no plans to visit the Superdome when he traveled to New Orleans in the summer of 2005. He was a violinist preparing for a major competition. Thompson came to the city to practice and be inspired by the large musical community there.

When he was forced to evacuate, Thompson had no car and nowhere to go except the Superdome. He strapped his violin case to his back and walked 1.5 miles (2.4 km) to the stadium, pulling his suitcases behind him. Thousands of others did the same.

◄ **The Superdome has hosted important events in New Orleans since 1975.**

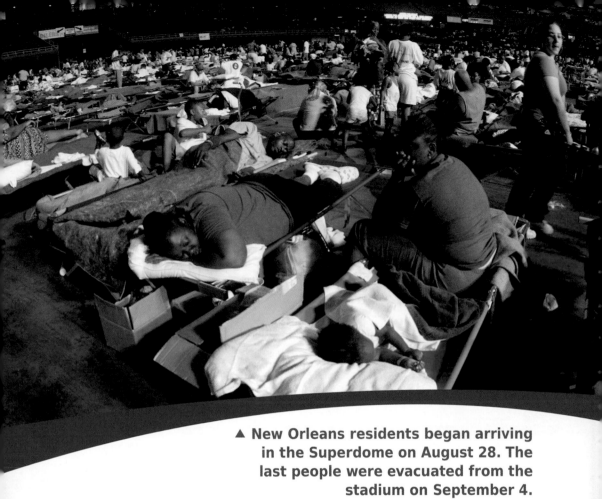

▲ **New Orleans residents began arriving in the Superdome on August 28. The last people were evacuated from the stadium on September 4.**

The people who shuffled into the Superdome that day had few choices. Many were poor, elderly, or sick. They had no way to get out of the city. They brought whatever belongings they could carry. Then, they staked out spots to wait out the storm.

Wind gusts rattled the building as Katrina roared **inland**. On the morning of August 29, the storm ripped two large holes in the Superdome roof. The stadium lost power. Thousands of people pressed together in near darkness. Without

air conditioning, the **humidity** was almost unbearable. As the
hours passed, conditions continued to get worse. Food was
scarce. Babies ran out of diapers. The toilets stopped flushing.
And still, more people kept coming.

FLOODING IN NEW ORLEANS

Bad flooding began in New Orleans on August 29. Levees
designed to keep water from entering the city failed due to
storm surges. In total, 80 percent of the city flooded. This map
shows the depth of water on September 3.

Depth (ft.)

| 0-1 |
| 1-2 |
| 2-3 |
| 3-4 |
| 4-5 |
| 5-6 |
| 6-7 |
| 7-8 |
| 8-9 |
| 9-10 |
| 10-15 |
| 15-20 |
| >20 |

USACE
Flood
Status
Zones

Zone
ID

Hurricane Katrina Flooding
Estimated Depth and Extent
03 September 2005

Fear and desperation seemed to bring out the worst in many. Soldiers tried to keep peace. But there were fights and robberies, and soon came sounds of gunfire.

By the end of the week, six people had died from natural causes in the Superdome. Two others drown outside the stadium. Through all the misery, Thompson waited with some of his friends who had also come to the stadium.

Suddenly, one of his friends suggested that Thompson start to play. Thompson took out his violin, his most precious possession. Standing beside a pile of trash, he began to play a piece by composer Johann Sebastian Bach.

The music cut through the hopelessness in the air. Thompson continued to play. "These people have nothing," he said. "I have a violin. And I should play for them. They should have something."[9]

◄ **The Superdome protected thousands from Hurricane Katrina. But conditions in the stadium became terrible following the storm.**

GLOSSARY

coastline (KOHST-line): Coastline is the area where the land meets the water. Hurricane Katrina did a lot of damage along the U.S. coastline in the Gulf of Mexico.

eye (eye): The eye is the middle part of a hurricane. The eye of a hurricane is often calm.

generator (JEN-uh-ray-tur): A generator is a machine that produces electricity. A generator can power an entire building.

humidity (hyoo-MID-i-tee): Humidity is the amount of moisture in the air. New Orleans has a high level of humidity in the summer.

inland (IN-luhnd): When something is inland, it is away from the sea. Hurricane Katrina traveled inland through Louisiana and Mississippi.

landfall (LAND-fawl): When a storm starts to move over land instead of water, it makes landfall. Hurricane Katrina first made landfall in Florida.

levees (LEV-eez): Levees are walls built to hold back floodwaters. The levees in New Orleans broke, flooding the city.

mandatory (MAN-duh-tor-ee): Something is mandatory if it is required. Officials said it was mandatory for people to leave New Orleans before the storm struck.

storm surge (storm surj): High waters caused by a storm create a storm surge. Water from the Hurricane Katrina storm surge trapped many residents in their homes.

SOURCE NOTES

1. Katy Reckdahl. "Boy Born a Day before Katrina 'Was Determined to be a New Orleans Baby.'" *The Times-Picayune.* NOLA Media Group, 27 Aug. 2010. Web. 14 Apr. 2015.

2. Ibid.

3. Ibid.

4. Sara Faulkner. "Katrina Oral History: AST3 Sara Faulkner." *U.S. Coast Guard Oral History Program.* U.S. Coast Guard, 4 Oct. 2005. Web. 14 Apr. 2015.

5. Stephanie Young. "Reflections on Katrina—AST2 Sara Faulkner." *Coast Guard Compass.* U.S. Coast Guard, 25 Aug. 2010. Web. 16 May 2015.

6. Ibid.

7. Douglas Brinkley. *The Great Deluge: Hurricane Katrina, New Orleans, and the Mississippi Gulf Coast.* New York: Morrow, 2006. Print. 152.

8. Associated Press. "Spindly Bush Proves Life-Saver in Miss. Town." *NBCNews.com.* NBC News Digital, 1 Sep. 2005. Web. 16 May 2015.

9. Scott Gold. "Trapped in an Arena of Suffering." *LATimes.com.* Los Angeles Times, 1 Sep. 2005. Web. 14 Apr. 2015.

TO LEARN MORE

Books

Benoit, Peter. *Hurricane Katrina*. New York: Scholastic, 2012.

Miller, Debra A. *Hurricane Katrina: Devastation on the Gulf Coast.* Detroit: Lucent Books, 2006.

Tarshis, Lauren. *I Survived Hurricane Katrina*, 2005. New York: Scholastic, 2011.

Web Sites

Visit our Web site for links about Hurricane Katrina: childsworld.com/links

Note to Parents, Teachers, and Librarians: We routinely verify our Web links to make sure they are safe and active sites. So encourage your readers to check them out!

INDEX